Deep River Dark

Story and Illustrations
by Dan Gremminger

Written by Bradley Harding

Rainy Day Press

To Purchase This Book Online:
www.zerogdanno.com/DeepRiverDark

ISBN 0-9778231-0-5

Copyright ©2006 Rainy Day Press

All rights reserved. No part of this book may be reproduced in any form or by any electronic or mechanical means, including information storage and retrieval systems, without permission in writing from the publisher, except by a reviewer who may quote brief passages in a review.

First Edition

Printed in China

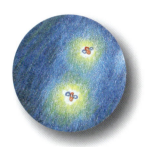

To Carolyn and Mike
and the Magic
of a Childhood Night

Home to them
A great divide
Sky of clouds
Low valley wide

Far away
The river bends
Calling out
Come my friends

Gathering
Family all
Following
Old river's call

Eyes aglow
Anticipate
Next day's catch
Morning's fate

Hooks and line
Worn hunter's knife
Jelly jars
For catching life

Box of bait

A tent, some spray

Sleeping bags

One night, one day

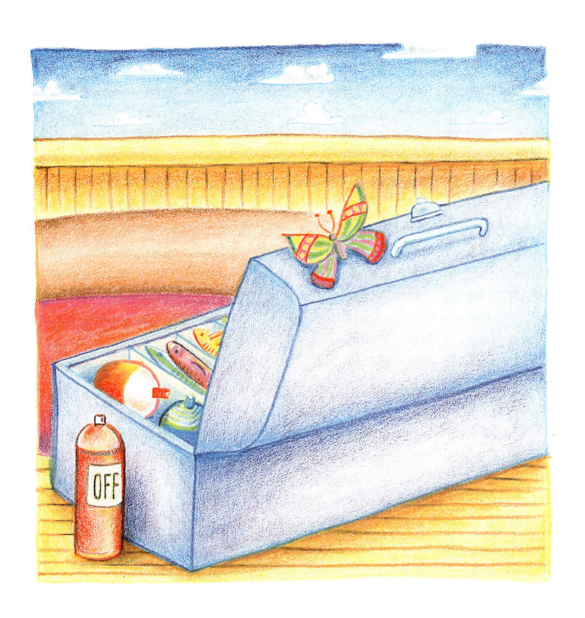

Bridge across
The river calm
Sun retires
Asleep till dawn

ather spins

A tale or two

Campfire ghost

A fish called Blue

Lost in thought
They fantasize
Catching Blue
A hunter's prize

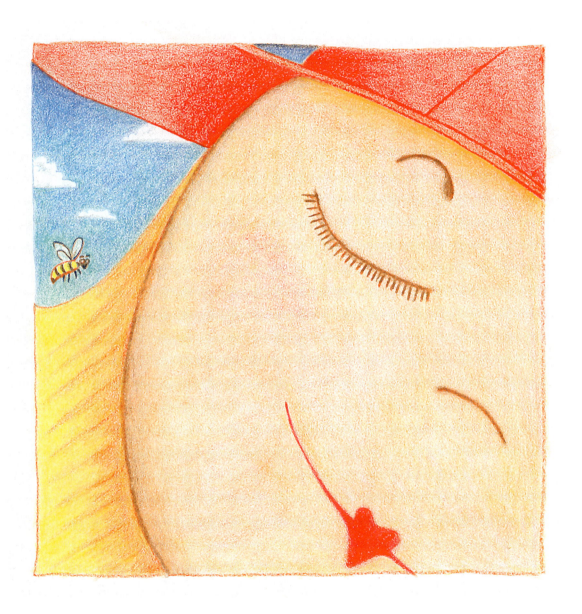

Evening camp
A river view
Sky of stars
Moon anew

Filled with life
The magic night
Theirs to keep
Lid on tight

Campfire flames
And songs of old
Dogs on sticks
Tales twice told

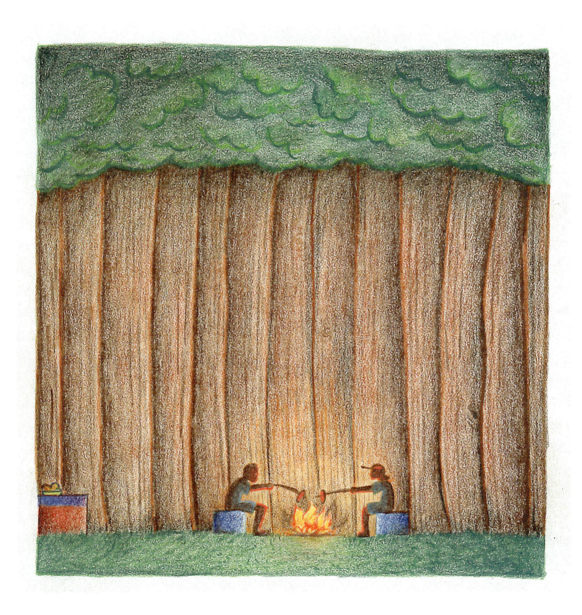

Flashlight beams
Dance through the sky
Moon beyond
Young dreamers fly

Light invites
Parade of life
Awakening
The tranquil night

Falling star
A simple wish
Catch they will
The fabled fish

Whispers plot
A voyage late
Row boat, poles
A net, some bait

Secretly
The darkness hides
Hunters three
Moonlight guides

Home to them
Perch, bass and carp
Full of life

Deep river dark

Baiting hooks
Three fishers boast
Which of them
Shall catch the most

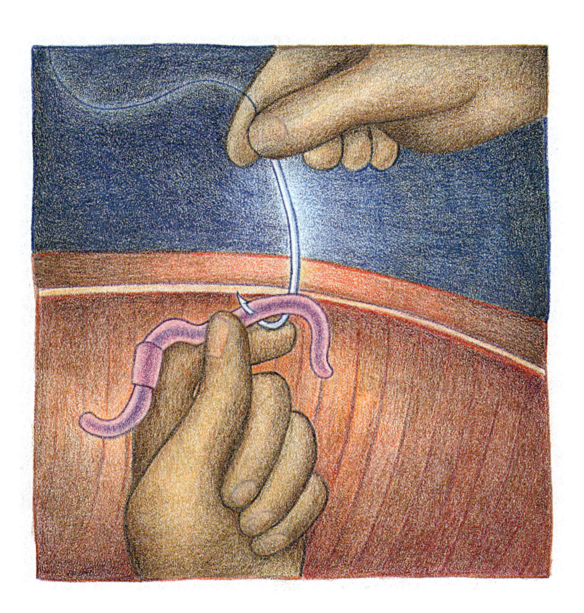

River still
None dares to say
A certain fish
Each hope to slay

Bobbing cork
Soon disappears
Underneath
Smooth surface clear

Suddenly
A pull below
Siblings hold
Not letting go

In their net
The hunters' prize
Blue, the fish
With human eyes

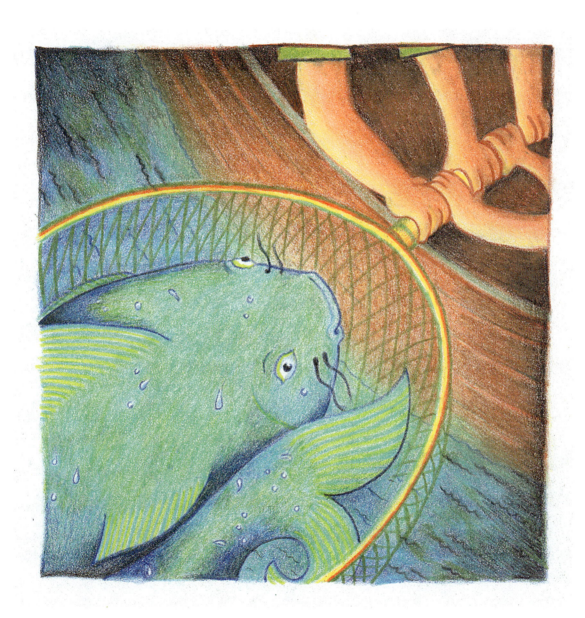

Let me live
He seems to say
Life's not yours
To take away

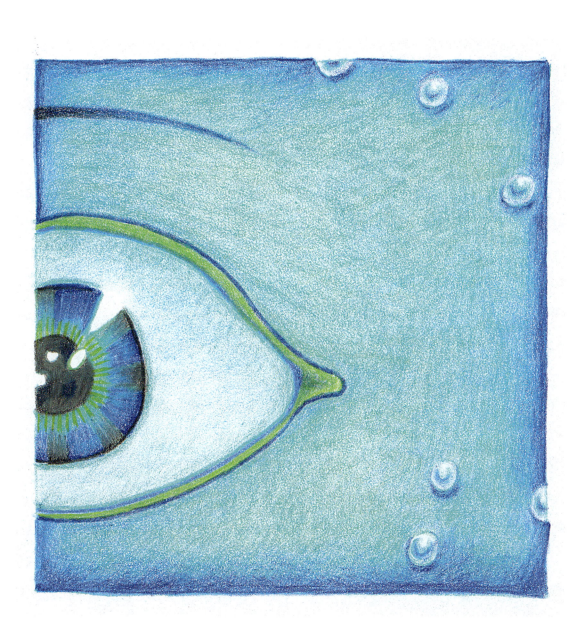

Quiet hush
Envelops all
As they hear
The river's call

All at once
The children three
Toss the net
And set Blue free

Crickets sing
An owl takes flight
Life surrounds
Bright peaceful night

Saving blue
And catching sleep
Life's to share
Not to keep